To

_____

From

_____

Date

_____

The joy of the Lord is your strength.

Nehemiah 8:10

The LORD is my shepherd, I shall not be in want.

~ *Psalm 23:1*

_____

_____

_____

_____

_____

_____

_____

_____

_____

_____

_____

_____

_____

_____

_____

_____

_____

_____

_____

_____

_____

_____

_____

_____

_____

In all things God works for the good of those who love Him,
who have been called according to His purpose.

~ Romans 8:28

The eternal God is your refuge,
and underneath are the everlasting arms.
~ *Deuteronomy 33:27*

_____

Be strong and courageous. Do not be terrified;
for the LORD your God will be with you wherever you go.

~ *Joshua 1:9*

You have made known to me the path of life; You will fill me with
joy in Your presence, with eternal pleasures at Your right hand.

~ Psalm 16:11

As for God, His way is perfect; the word of the LORD is flawless. He is a shield for all who take refuge in Him.

~ 2 Samuel 22:31

Ascribe to the LORD the glory due His name. Bring an offering and come before Him; worship the LORD in the splendor of His holiness.

~ 1 Chronicles 16:29

The joy of the LORD is your strength.
~ Nehemiah 8:10

He will yet fill your mouth with
laughter and your lips with shouts of joy.
~ Job 8:21

O Lord, our Lord, how majestic is Your name in all the earth!
~ Psalm 8:9

The LORD will watch over your coming
and going both now and forevermore.
~ Psalm 121:8

_____

The heavens declare the glory of God;
the skies proclaim the work of His hands.
~ Psalm 19:1

The Lord is my light and my salvation – whom shall I fear?
The Lord is the stronghold of my life – of whom shall I be afraid?

~ *Psalm 27:1*

One thing I ask of the LORD, this is what I seek: that I may
dwell in the house of the LORD all the days of my life.

~ Psalm 27:4

Taste and see that the LORD is good;
blessed is the man who takes refuge in Him.
~ *Psalm 34:8*

_____

God has made everything beautiful in its time.
~ *Ecclesiastes 3:11*

_____

_____
_____
_____
_____
_____
_____
_____
_____
_____
_____
_____
_____
_____
_____
_____
_____
_____
_____
_____
_____
_____
_____
_____
_____
_____
_____

Praise be to the God and Father of our Lord Jesus Christ,
who has blessed us with every spiritual blessing in Christ.

~ Ephesians 1:3

Finally, be strong in the Lord and in His mighty power.
~ *Ephesians 6:10*

Rejoice in the Lord always. I will say it again: Rejoice!
~ Philippians 4:4

Christ in you, the hope of glory.
~ Colossians 1:27

Now faith is being sure of what we hope
for and certain of what we do not see.

~ Hebrews 11:1

_____

"Do not let your hearts be troubled. Trust in God; trust also in Me."

~ John 14:1

_____

_____

_____

_____

_____

_____

_____

_____

_____

_____

_____

_____

_____

_____

_____

_____

_____

_____

_____

_____

_____

_____

_____

_____

_____

_____

"Let your light shine before men, that they may see
your good deeds and praise your Father in heaven."

~ *Matthew 5:16*

_____

"Blessed are those who hunger and thirst
for righteousness, for they will be filled."
~ Matthew 5:6

_____

_____
_____
_____
_____
_____
_____
_____
_____
_____
_____
_____
_____
_____
_____
_____
_____
_____
_____
_____
_____
_____
_____
_____
_____
_____
_____
_____
_____

"But seek first His kingdom and His righteousness,
and all these things will be given to you as well."
~ Matthew 6:33

_____

_____

"Ask and it will be given to you; seek and you will find;
knock and the door will be opened to you."

~ Matthew 7:7

_____

_____
_____
_____
_____
_____
_____
_____
_____
_____
_____
_____
_____
_____
_____
_____
_____
_____
_____
_____
_____
_____
_____
_____
_____

From the fullness of His grace we have
all received one blessing after another.
~ John 1:16

_____

Shout for joy to the LORD, all the earth.
~ *Psalm 100:1*

Come, let us sing for joy to the LORD; let us
shout aloud to the Rock of our salvation.

~ Psalm 95:1

_____

How many are Your works, O LORD! In wisdom You
made them all; the earth is full of Your creatures.

~ Psalm 104:24

The fear of the LORD is the beginning of wisdom;
all who follow His precepts have good understanding.

_____

You will keep in perfect peace him whose
mind is steadfast, because he trusts in You.
~ Isaiah 26:3

The Lord is my shepherd, I shall not be in want.
~ Psalm 23:1

In all things God works for the good of those who love Him,
who have been called according to His purpose.

~ *Romans 8:28*

The eternal God is your refuge,
and underneath are the everlasting arms.
~ Deuteronomy 33:27

_____

‌

Be strong and courageous. Do not be terrified;
for the LORD your God will be with you wherever you go.
~ *Joshua 1:9*

_____

_____
_____
_____
_____
_____
_____
_____
_____
_____
_____
_____
_____
_____
_____
_____
_____
_____
_____
_____
_____
_____
_____
_____
_____
_____
_____
_____
_____
_____
_____

You have made known to me the path of life; You will fill me with
joy in Your presence, with eternal pleasures at Your right hand.

~ Psalm 16:11

_____

As for God, His way is perfect; the word of the LORD is
flawless. He is a shield for all who take refuge in Him.
~ 2 Samuel 22:31

Ascribe to the LORD the glory due His name. Bring an offering and come before Him; worship the LORD in the splendor of His holiness.

~ 1 Chronicles 16:29

_____

The joy of the Lord is your strength.
~ *Nehemiah 8:10*

He will yet fill your mouth with
laughter and your lips with shouts of joy.
~ *Job 8:21*

_____

O Lᴏʀᴅ, our Lord, how majestic is Your name in all the earth!
~ Psalm 8:9

The LORD will watch over your coming
and going both now and forevermore.

~ Psalm 121:8

The heavens declare the glory of God;
the skies proclaim the work of His hands.

~ Psalm 19:1

_____

_____
_____
_____
_____
_____
_____
_____
_____
_____
_____
_____
_____
_____
_____
_____
_____
_____
_____
_____
_____
_____
_____
_____
_____
_____
_____

The LORD is my light and my salvation – whom shall I fear?
The LORD is the stronghold of my life – of whom shall I be afraid?

~ Psalm 27:1

_____

One thing I ask of the LORD, this is what I seek: that I may
dwell in the house of the LORD all the days of my life.

~ Psalm 27:4

Taste and see that the LORD is good;
blessed is the man who takes refuge in Him.

~ Psalm 34:8

_____

God has made everything beautiful in its time.

~ *Ecclesiastes 3:11*

_____

_____

_____

_____

_____

_____

_____

_____

_____

_____

_____

_____

_____

_____

_____

_____

_____

_____

_____

_____

_____

_____

_____

_____

_____

_____

_____

_____

_____

Praise be to the God and Father of our Lord Jesus Christ,
who has blessed us with every spiritual blessing in Christ.

~ Ephesians 1:3

Finally, be strong in the Lord and in His mighty power.
~ *Ephesians 6:10*

Rejoice in the Lord always. I will say it again: Rejoice!
~ Philippians 4:4

_____

Christ in you, the hope of glory.
~ *Colossians 1:27*

Now faith is being sure of what we hope
for and certain of what we do not see.

_____

"Do not let your hearts be troubled. Trust in God; trust also in Me."
~ *John 14:1*

_____

_____

_____

_____

_____

_____

_____

_____

_____

_____

_____

_____

_____

_____

_____

_____

_____

_____

_____

_____

_____

_____

_____

_____

_____

_____

"Let your light shine before men, that they may see
your good deeds and praise your Father in heaven."

~ *Matthew 5:16*

"Blessed are those who hunger and thirst
for righteousness, for they will be filled."

~ Matthew 5:6

_____

_____

_____

_____

_____

_____

_____

_____

_____

_____

_____

_____

_____

_____

_____

_____

_____

_____

_____

_____

_____

_____

_____

_____

_____

"But seek first His kingdom and His righteousness,
and all these things will be given to you as well."

~ *Matthew 6:33*

_____

"Ask and it will be given to you; seek and you will find;
knock and the door will be opened to you."
~ Matthew 7:7

From the fullness of His grace we have
all received one blessing after another.
~ John 1:16

_____

Shout for joy to the LORD, all the earth.

~ Psalm 100:1

Come, let us sing for joy to the LORD; let us
shout aloud to the Rock of our salvation.

~ *Psalm 95:1*

How many are Your works, O Lord! In wisdom You
made them all; the earth is full of Your creatures.

~ Psalm 104:24

The fear of the LORD is the beginning of wisdom;
all who follow His precepts have good understanding.

~ Psalm 111:10

_____

You will keep in perfect peace him whose
mind is steadfast, because he trusts in You.

~ Isaiah 26:3

The LORD is my shepherd, I shall not be in want.

~ Psalm 23:1

_____

In all things God works for the good of those who love Him,
who have been called according to His purpose.

~ Romans 8:28

_____

_____

_____

_____

_____

_____

_____

_____

_____

_____

_____

_____

_____

_____

_____

_____

_____

_____

_____

_____

_____

_____

_____

_____

_____

_____

The eternal God is your refuge,
and underneath are the everlasting arms.
~ Deuteronomy 33:27

_____

Be strong and courageous. Do not be terrified;
for the LORD your God will be with you wherever you go.

~ Joshua 1:9

You have made known to me the path of life; You will fill me with
joy in Your presence, with eternal pleasures at Your right hand.

~ *Psalm 16:11*

As for God, His way is perfect; the word of the LORD is flawless. He is a shield for all who take refuge in Him.

~ 2 Samuel 22:31

Ascribe to the LORD the glory due His name. Bring an offering and come before Him; worship the LORD in the splendor of His holiness.

~ *1 Chronicles 16:29*

The joy of the LORD is your strength.
~ *Nehemiah 8:10*

He will yet fill your mouth with
laughter and your lips with shouts of joy.

~ Job 8:21

_____

O LORD, our Lord, how majestic is Your name in all the earth!
~ Psalm 8:9

The LORD will watch over your coming
and going both now and forevermore.

~ Psalm 121:8

_____

The heavens declare the glory of God;
the skies proclaim the work of His hands.

~ *Psalm 19:1*

The LORD is my light and my salvation – whom shall I fear?
The LORD is the stronghold of my life – of whom shall I be afraid?

~ Psalm 27:1

_____

One thing I ask of the LORD, this is what I seek: that I may
dwell in the house of the LORD all the days of my life.

~ *Psalm 27:4*

Taste and see that the LORD is good;
blessed is the man who takes refuge in Him.

~ Psalm 34:8

_____

God has made everything beautiful in its time.

~ *Ecclesiastes 3:11*

_____

_____

_____

_____

_____

_____

_____

_____

_____

_____

_____

_____

_____

_____

_____

_____

_____

_____

_____

_____

_____

_____

_____

_____

_____

_____

_____

Praise be to the God and Father of our Lord Jesus Christ,
who has blessed us with every spiritual blessing in Christ.

~ *Ephesians 1:3*

Finally, be strong in the Lord and in His mighty power.

~ *Ephesians 6:10*

Rejoice in the Lord always. I will say it again: Rejoice!

~ Philippians 4:4

_____

Christ in you, the hope of glory.
~ *Colossians 1:27*

Now faith is being sure of what we hope
for and certain of what we do not see.

~ Hebrews 11:1

"Do not let your hearts be troubled. Trust in God; trust also in Me."

~ John 14:1

"Let your light shine before men, that they may see
your good deeds and praise your Father in heaven."
~ Matthew 5:16

_____

"Blessed are those who hunger and thirst
for righteousness, for they will be filled."
~ Matthew 5:6

_____

_____
_____
_____
_____
_____
_____
_____
_____
_____
_____
_____
_____
_____
_____
_____
_____
_____
_____
_____
_____
_____
_____
_____
_____
_____
_____
_____

"But seek first His kingdom and His righteousness,
and all these things will be given to you as well."
~ Matthew 6:33

_____

"Ask and it will be given to you; seek and you will find;
knock and the door will be opened to you."

~ Matthew 7:7

From the fullness of His grace we have
all received one blessing after another.
~ John 1:16

Shout for joy to the LORD, all the earth.

~ Psalm 100:1

Come, let us sing for joy to the LORD; let us
shout aloud to the Rock of our salvation.

~ *Psalm 95:1*

_____

How many are Your works, O Lord! In wisdom You
made them all; the earth is full of Your creatures.

~ Psalm 104:24

The fear of the LORD is the beginning of wisdom;
all who follow His precepts have good understanding.

~ Psalm 111:10

You will keep in perfect peace him whose
mind is steadfast, because he trusts in You.
~ Isaiah 26:3

The LORD is my shepherd, I shall not be in want.

~ Psalm 23:1

_____

In all things God works for the good of those who love Him,
who have been called according to His purpose.
~ Romans 8:28

The eternal God is your refuge,
and underneath are the everlasting arms.
~ *Deuteronomy 33:27*

_____

Be strong and courageous. Do not be terrified;
for the LORD your God will be with you wherever you go.

~ Joshua 1:9

_____

_____
_____
_____
_____
_____
_____
_____
_____
_____
_____
_____
_____
_____
_____
_____
_____
_____
_____
_____
_____
_____
_____
_____
_____
_____
_____

You have made known to me the path of life; You will fill me with
joy in Your presence, with eternal pleasures at Your right hand.

~ *Psalm 16:11*

As for God, His way is perfect; the word of the LORD is
flawless. He is a shield for all who take refuge in Him.

~ 2 Samuel 22:31

Ascribe to the LORD the glory due His name. Bring an offering and come before Him; worship the LORD in the splendor of His holiness.

~ 1 Chronicles 16:29

The joy of the LORD is your strength.
~ Nehemiah 8:10

He will yet fill your mouth with
laughter and your lips with shouts of joy.
~ Job 8:21

_____

O LORD, our Lord, how majestic is Your name in all the earth!
~ Psalm 8:9

The LORD will watch over your coming
and going both now and forevermore.
                                    ~ Psalm 121:8

_____

The heavens declare the glory of God;
the skies proclaim the work of His hands.

~ *Psalm 19:1*

The Lord is my light and my salvation – whom shall I fear?
The Lord is the stronghold of my life – of whom shall I be afraid?

~ Psalm 27:1

_____

One thing I ask of the LORD, this is what I seek: that I may
dwell in the house of the LORD all the days of my life.

~ *Psalm 27:4*

Taste and see that the Lord is good;
blessed is the man who takes refuge in Him.
~ Psalm 34:8

_____

God has made everything beautiful in its time.
~ *Ecclesiastes 3:11*

_____

_____
_____
_____
_____
_____
_____
_____
_____
_____
_____
_____
_____
_____
_____
_____
_____
_____
_____
_____
_____
_____
_____
_____
_____
_____

Praise be to the God and Father of our Lord Jesus Christ,
who has blessed us with every spiritual blessing in Christ.

~ Ephesians 1:3

Finally, be strong in the Lord and in His mighty power.

Rejoice in the Lord always. I will say it again: Rejoice!

~ Philippians 4:4

Christ in you, the hope of glory.
~ *Colossians 1:27*

Now faith is being sure of what we hope
for and certain of what we do not see.

~ *Hebrews 11:1*

_____

"Do not let your hearts be troubled. Trust in God; trust also in Me."

~ *John 14:1*

_____

_____

_____

_____

_____

_____

_____

_____

_____

_____

_____

_____

_____

_____

_____

_____

_____

_____

_____

_____

_____

_____

_____

_____

_____

_____

_____

"Let your light shine before men, that they may see
your good deeds and praise your Father in heaven."

~ *Matthew 5:16*

_____

"Blessed are those who hunger and thirst
for righteousness, for they will be filled."

~ Matthew 5:6

_____

_____
_____
_____
_____
_____
_____
_____
_____
_____
_____
_____
_____
_____
_____
_____
_____
_____
_____
_____
_____
_____
_____
_____
_____
_____
_____
_____
_____
_____
_____

"But seek first His kingdom and His righteousness,
and all these things will be given to you as well."
~ *Matthew 6:33*

_____

_____

_____

_____

_____

_____

_____

_____

_____

_____

_____

_____

_____

_____

_____

_____

_____

_____

_____

_____

_____

_____

_____

"Ask and it will be given to you; seek and you will find;
knock and the door will be opened to you."

~ Matthew 7:7

From the fullness of His grace we have
all received one blessing after another.
~ John 1:16

_____

_____
_____
_____
_____
_____
_____
_____
_____
_____
_____
_____
_____
_____
_____
_____
_____
_____
_____
_____
_____
_____
_____
_____
_____
_____
_____

Shout for joy to the LORD, all the earth.
~ Psalm 100:1

Come, let us sing for joy to the LORD; let us
shout aloud to the Rock of our salvation.

~ Psalm 95:1

How many are Your works, O Lord! In wisdom You
made them all; the earth is full of Your creatures.

~ Psalm 104:24